How Can My Community Improve?

TAKING CIVIC ACTION

Mitchell Allen

CIVICS FOR THE REAL WORLD™

Rosen Classroom™

Published in 2019 by The Rosen Publishing Group, Inc.
29 East 21st Street, New York, NY 10010

Book Design: Rachel Rising
Editor: Ryan Wolf

Photo Credits: Cover, p. 14 Sergey Novikov/Shutterstock.com; pp. 4, 12 Rawpixel.com/Shutterstock.com; p. 7 EvgeniiAnd/Shutterstock.com;
p. 8 Dmytro Zinkevych/Shutterstock.com; p. 11 robert_s/Shutterstock.com.

ISBN: 9781538365755
6-pack ISBN: 9781538365762

Manufactured in the United States of America

CPSIA Compliance Information: Batch #WS18RC: For Further Information contact Rosen Publishing, New York, New York at 1-800-237-9932

CONTENTS

MAKING THINGS BETTER

If you could change anything about your community, what would it be? Would you make things safer for kids and adults? Do some places need to be cleaned up or fixed? Do some people or animals need help?

These are just some of the many questions you could ask yourself. All change, big or small, has to start somewhere. Maybe it could start with you! Even if you want to change lots of things, it's best to pick one thing to start with.

WHERE TO START

You don't want to do more than you can handle! Maybe you could shovel snow for your older neighbors when the weather is bad. You could also offer to walk pets or take out garbage. Others might really need the help.

Even one person can still help a few people. Do you have any ideas?

WORKING TOGETHER

You might find there are more people who need help than you can safely **assist**. You could get a group of friends together to help them.

Maybe your school would let you start a community service club. Working together, people can do a lot more than they could do alone. One person can help when another person is busy with homework or other activities. People who work together can do things much faster!

ASKING FOR HELP

You won't be able to fix every problem yourself. Even a team of friends working together might not be able to improve things!

Maybe people are driving really fast down your street and it's becoming **dangerous**. That's when it's important to ask for help. Maybe your local police department can watch for this problem. Or maybe you can write to other officials to see if they can change the speed limit.

STAND UP FOR CHANGE

Sometimes it takes lots of work to improve something or to fix a problem. You'll need lots of people to join together to ask for change.

You can start a **petition** or get a group together to speak at a community meeting. It's harder to **ignore** a problem when lots of people speak up about it! You can keep reminding people in power that you won't go away.

KEEP WORKING

Even if your community improvements take time, keep working for them. Change sometimes happens very slowly. Don't forget about what is important to you, but don't get **discouraged** either.

Every good change in the world started somewhere. Both big changes and small changes all started with people just like you! You can make your community — and the world — a better place if you don't give up.

GLOSSARY

assist: Help.

dangerous: Unsafe.

discourage: To make someone less hopeful or less sure of himself or herself.

ignore: To pay no attention to.

petition: A written request, or question, asking a government or person to do something.

INDEX